HOW TO ATTRACT MONEY

Dr. Joseph Murphy

Pharos Books

ISBN: 978-93-58049-56-5
eISBN: 978-93-58049-37-4

Publisher: Pharos Books (P) Ltd.
Plot No.-55, Main Mother Dairy Road
Pandav Nagar, East Delhi-110092
Phone: 011-40395855, +14049995474
WhatsApp: +91 8368220032
E-mail: sales@pharosbooks.in
Website: www.pharosbooks.in
First Edition: 2023

How to Attract Money
Dr. Joseph Murphy

Contents

Preface 5
Your Right to Be Rich 7
The Road to Riches 29
About Dr. Joseph Murphy 52

Preface

Murphy writes that "it is your right to be rich. You are here to lead the abundant life, and to be happy, radiant and free. You should, therefore, have all the money you need to lead a full, happy and prosperous life.... Wealth is a state of consciousness; it is a mind conditioned to Divine supply forever flowing.

Money is only a symbol; it has taken many forms as a medium of exchange down through the centuries, such as salt, beads, or various trinkets. In early times, man's wealth was determined by the number of sheep or oxen he had. It is much more convenient to write a check than to carry some sheep around with you to pay your bills. God does not want you to live in a hovel or to go hungry. God wants you to be happy, prosperous, and successful. God is always successful in all His undertakings, whether He makes a star or a cosmos!

Riches are of the mind. Let us suppose for a moment that a physician's diploma was stolen together with his office equipment. I am sure you would agree that his wealth was in his mind. He could still carry on, diagnose disease, prescribe, operate, and lecture on materia medica. Only his symbols were stolen; he could always get additional supplies. His riches were in his mental capacity, knowledge to help others, and his ability to contribute to humanity in general.

'Every man at the beginning doth set forth good wine; and when men have well drunk, then that which is worse; but thou hast kept the good wine until now.' This is true of every man when he first enters a knowledge of the laws of the mind. He sets out with high spirits and ambitions. He is the new broom which sweeps clean, and he is full of good intentions; oftentimes he forgets the Source of power. He does not remain faithful to the Principle within him, which is scientific and effectual, that would lift him out of his negative experiences and set him on the high road to freedom and peace of mind. He begins to indulge mentally and emotionally with ideas and thoughts extraneous to his announced aim and goal. In other words, he is not faithful to his ideal or wife.

Dr Joseph Murphy was a proponent of the New Thought movement. This movement was developed in the late 19th and early 20th centuries by many philosophers and deep thinkers who studied this phenomenon and preached, wrote, and practiced a new way of looking at life. By combining a metaphysical, spiritual, and pragmatic approach to the way we think and live, they uncovered the secret of attaining what we truly desire.

Murphy has a gift for expressing great truths in a clear manner. If you are a hard worker but simply can't seem to get ahead, this book will change your life. As always, Murphy includes specific examples of what people can achieve if they start using their imaginative intelligence. These examples will inspire you to try out his methods for yourself.

—*Roger Fritz*

Your Right to Be Rich

It is your right to be rich. You are here to lead the abundant life, to be happy, radiant, and free. You should, therefore, have all the money you need to lead a full, happy, prosperous life.

There is no virtue in poverty; the latter is a mental disease. It should be abolished from the face of the earth. You are here to grow, expand, and unfold- spiritually, mentally, and materially.

You have the inalienable right to fully develop and express yourself along all lines. You should surround yourself with beauty and luxury.

Why be satisfied with just enough to go around when you can enjoy the riches of the Infinite? In this book you will learn to make friends with money, and you will always have a surplus. Your desire to be rich is a desire for a fuller, happier, more wonderful life. It is a cosmic urge. It is good—very good.

Begin to see money in its true significance: as a symbol of exchange. It means to you freedom from want; it means beauty, luxury, abundance, as also refinement. As you read this chapter, you are probably saying, 'I want more money.' 'I am worthy of a higher salary than I am receiving.

I believe most people are inadequately compensated. One of the reasons many people do not have more money is that they are silently or openly condemning it. They refer to money as 'filthy lucre,' or they believe that 'Love of money is the root of all evil,' etc. Another reason they do not prosper is that they have a sneaky, subconscious feeling there is some virtue in poverty; this subconscious pattern may be due to early childhood training, superstition, or it could be based on a false interpretation of the scriptures.

There is no virtue in poverty; it is a disease like any other mental disease. If you were physically ill, you would think there was something wrong with you; you would seek help, or do something about the condition at once. Likewise, if you do not have money constantly circulating in your life, there is something radically wrong with you.

Money is only a symbol; it has taken many forms as a medium of exchange down through the centuries, such as salt, beads, or various trinkets. In early times, man's wealth was determined by the number of sheep or oxen he had. It is much more convenient to write a check than to carry some sheep around with you to pay your bills.

God does not want you to live in a hovel or to go hungry. God wants you to be happy, prosperous, and successful. God is always successful in all His undertakings, whether He makes a star or a cosmos!

You may wish to take a trip around the world, study art in foreign countries, go to college, or send your children to a superior school. You certainly wish to bring up your children in lovely surroundings, so that they might learn to appreciate beauty, order, symmetry, and proportion.

You were born to succeed, to win, to conquer all difficulties, and to have all your faculties fully developed. If there is financial lack in your life, do something about it.

Get away immediately from all superstitious beliefs about money. Do not ever regard money as evil or filthy. If you do, you cause it to take wings to fly away from you. Remember that you lose what you condemn.

Suppose, for example, you found gold, silver, lead, copper, or iron in the ground. Would you pronounce these things evil? God pronounced all things good. The evil comes from man's darkened understanding, from his unenlightened mind, from his false interpretation of life, and his misuse of Divine Power.

Uranium, lead, or some other metal could have been used as a medium of exchange. We use paper bills, checks, etc.; surely the piece of paper is not evil; neither is the check. Physicists as also other scientists know today that the only difference between ometals is the number and rate of motion of the electrons revolving around a central nucleus. They are now changing one metal into another through a bombardment of the atoms in the powerful cyclotron. Gold under certain conditions becomes mercury. It will be only a little while until gold, silver, and other metals will be made synthetically in the chemical laboratory. I cannot imagine seeing anything evil in electrons, neutrons, protons, and isotopes.

The piece of paper in your pocket is composed of electrons as well as protons arranged differently; their number and rate of motion is different; that is the only way the paper differs from the silver in your pocket.

Some people will say, 'Oh, people kill for money. They steal for money!' It has been associated with countless crimes, but that does not make it evil.

Anyone may give another person $50 to kill someone; they has misused money to use it for a destructive purpose. You can use electricity to kill someone or to light the house. You can use water to quench the baby's thirst, or use it to drown the child. You can use fire to warm the child, or burn it to death.

Another illustration would be if you brought some soil from your garden and put it in your coffee cup for breakfast: that would be your evil; yet the earth is not evil; neither is the coffee. The soil is misplaced; it belongs in your garden.

Similarly, if a needle were stuck in your thumb, it would be your evil; the needle or pin belongs in the pin cushion, not in your thumb. It is useful and good as an instrument, a tool to sew.

We know the forces or the elements of nature are not evil; it depends on our use of them whether they bless or hurt us.

A man said to me one time, 'I am broke. I do not like money; it is the root of all evil.'

Love of money to the exclusion of everything else will cause you to become lopsided a indeed unbalanced. You are here to use your power or authority wisely. Some men crave power; others crave money. If you set your heart on money, and say, "'That is all I want. I am going to give all my attention to amassing money; nothing else matters,' you can get money and attain a fortune, but you have forgotten that you are here to lead a balanced life. 'Man does not live by bread alone.'

For example, if you belong to some cult, or religious group, and become fanatical about it, excluding yourself from your friends, society, and social activities, you will become unbalanced, inhibited—frustrated as well. Nature insists on a balance. If all your time is devoted to external things and possessions, you will find yourself hungry for peace of mind, harmony, love, joy, or perfect health. You will find that you cannot buy anything that is real. You can amass a fortune, or have millions of dollars; this is not evil or bad. Love of money to the exclusion of everything else results in frustration, disappointment, as also disillusionment; in that sense it is the root of your evil.

By making money your sole aim, you simply made a wrong choice. You thought that was all you wanted, but you found after all your efforts that it was not only the money you needed. What you really desired was true place, peace of mind, with abundance. You could have the million or many millions, if you wanted them, yet still have peace of mind, harmony, perfect health, and Divine expression.

Everyone wants enough money, not just enough to go around. Surely those who want abundance and to spare; he should have it. The urges, desires, and impulses we have for food, clothing, homes, better means of transportation, expression, procreation,—abundance are all God-given, Divine, and good. Yet we may misdirect these impulses, desires, and urges, resulting in evil or negative experiences in our lives.

Man does not have an evil nature; there is no evil nature in you; it is God, the Universal Wisdom, or Life seeking expression through you.

For example, a boy wants to go to college, but he does not have enough money. He sees other boys in the neighborhood going off to college and the university; his desire increases. He says to himself, 'I want an education, too. Such a youth may steal or embezzle money for the purpose of going to college. The desire to go to college was basically and fundamentally good; he misdirected that desire or urge by violating the laws of society, the cosmic law of harmony, or the golden rule; then he finds himself in trouble.

However, if this boy knew the laws of mind, and his unqualified capacity through the use of the Spiritual Power to go to college, he would be free and not in jail. Who put him in jail? He placed himself there. The policeman who locked him up in prison was an instrument of the man made laws which he violated. He first imprisoned himself in his mind by stealing and hurting others. Fear and a guilt consciousness followed; this is the prison of the mind, followed by the prison walls made of bricks and stones.

Money is a symbol of God's opulence, beauty, refinement, and abundance. It should be used wisely, judiciously, and constructively to bless humanity in countless ways. It is merely a symbol of the economic health of the nation. When your blood is circulating freely, you are healthy. When money is circulating freely in your life, you are economically healthy. When people begin to hoard money, to put it away in tin boxes or become charged with fear, there is economic illness.

The crash of 1929 was a psychological panic: It was fear seizing the minds of people everywhere. It was a sort of negative, hypnotic spell. You are living in a subjective and objective world. You must not neglect the spiritual food, such as peace of mind, love, beauty, harmony, joy, and laughter.

Knowledge of the spiritual power is the means to the Royal Road to Riches of all kinds, whether your desire is spiritual, mental, or material. The student of the laws of mind, or the student of the spiritual principle, believes and knows absolutely that regardless of the economic situation, stock market fluctuation, depression, strikes, war, or other conditions and circumstances, he will always be amply supplied regardless of what form money may take.

The reason for this is he abides in the consciousness of wealth. The student has convinced himself in his mind that wealth is forever flowing freely in his life and there is always a Wealth is a state of consciousness; it is a mind conditioned to Divine supply forever flowing. The scientific thinker looks at money or wealth like the tide; i.e., it goes out, but it always comes back.

The tides never fail; neither will man's supply when he trusts a tireless, changeless, immortal Omnipresent Presence that flows ceaselessly. The man who knows the workings of the subconscious mind is never, therefore, worried about the economic situation, stock market panics, devaluation, or inflation of currency, since he abides in the consciousness of God's eternal supply. Such a man is always supplied and watched over by an over-shadowing Presence. "Behold the birds of the air: for they sow not, neither do they reap, nor gather into barns; yet your heavenly Father feeds them. Are you not much better than they?

Divine surplus. Should there be a war tomorrow to make valueless all the student's present holdings, as the German marks did after the First World War, he would still attract wealth. He would be cared for, regardless of the form of the new currency.

As you consciously commune with the Divine Presence, claiming and knowing that It leads and guides you in all your ways, that It is a Lamp unto your feet, and a Light on your path, you will be Divinely prospered and sustained beyond your wildest dreams.

Here is a simple way for you to impress your subconscious mind with the idea of constant supply or wealth: Quiet the wheels of your mind. Relax! Let go! Immobilize the attention. Get into a sleepy, drowsy, meditative state of mind; this reduces effort to the minimum; then, in a quiet, relaxed, passive way, reflect on the following simple truths: Ask yourself where do ideas come from? Where does wealth come from? Where did you come from? Where did your brain and your mind come from? You will be led back to the One Source.

You find yourself on a spiritual, working basis now. It will no longer insult your intelligence to realize that wealth is a state of mind.

Take this little phrase; repeat it slowly four or five minutes three or four times a day quietly to yourself, particularly before you go to sleep: 'Money is forever circulating freely in my life, and there is always a Divine surplus. As you do this regularly and systematically, the idea of wealth will be conveyed to your deeper mind, and you will develop a wealth consciousness. Idle, mechanical repetition will not succeed in building the consciousness of wealth. Begin to feel the truth of what you affirm. You know what you are doing, and why you are doing it. You know your deeper self is responsive to what you consciously accept as true.

In the beginning, people who are in financial difficulties do not get results with such affirmations as, 'I am wealthy,' 'I am prosperous,' 'I am successful'; such statements may cause their conditions to get worse. The reason is the subconscious mind will only accept the dominant of two ideas, or the dominant mood or feeling. When they say, 'I am prosperous,' their feeling of lack is greater, and something within them says, 'No, you are not prosperous, you are broke.'

The feeling of lack is dominant, so that each affirmation calls forth the mood of lack, and more lack becomes theirs. The way to overcome this for beginners is to affirm what the conscious and subconscious mind will agree on; then there will be no contradiction. Our subconscious mind accepts our beliefs, feelings, convictions, and what we consciously accept as true.

A man could engage the cooperation of his subconscious mind by saying, 'I am prospering every day.' 'I am growing in wealth and in wisdom every day. Every day my wealth is multiplying.' 'I am advancing, growing, and moving forward financially. These with other similar statements would not create any conflict in the mind.

For instance, if a salesman has only ten cents in his pocket, he could easily agree that he could have more tomorrow. If he sold a pair of shoes tomorrow, there is nothing within him which says his sales could not increase. He could use statements, such as, 'My sales are increasing every day.' 'I am advancing and moving forward. He would find these would be sound psychologically and acceptable to his mind. They would produce desirable fruit.

The spiritually advanced students who quietly, knowingly, and feelingly say, 'I am prosperous,' 'I am successful,' 'I am wealthy,' get wonderful results also. Why would this be true? When they think, feel, or say, 'I am prosperous,' they mean God is All Supply or Infinite Riches, and what is true of God is true of them. When they say, 'I am wealthy,' they know God is Infinite Supply, the Inexhaustible Treasure-House, and what is true of God is, therefore, true of them, for God is within them.

Many men get wonderful results by dwelling on three abstract ideas, such as health, wealth, and success. Health is a Divine Reality or quality of God. Wealth is of God; it is eternal as also endless. Success is of God; God is always successful in all His undertakings.

The way they produce remarkable results is to stand before a mirror as they shave, to repeat for five or ten minutes: 'Health, wealth, and success. They do not say, 'I am healthy,' or 'I am successful; they create no opposition in their minds.

They are quiet and relaxed; when the mind is receptive and passive. At that time, they repeat these words. Amazing results follow. All they are doing is identifying with truths that are eternal, changeless, and timeless.

You can develop a wealth consciousness. Put the principles enunciated as well as elaborated on in this book into practice. Your erstwhile desert will rejoice to blossom as the rose.

I worked with a young boy in Australia many years ago who wanted to become a physician and surgeon, but he had no money; nor had he graduated from high school. For expenses, he used to clean doctors' offices, wash windows, and do odd repair jobs. He told me that every night as he went to sleep, he used to see a diploma on a wall with his name in big, bold letters. He used to clean and shine the diplomas in the medical building where he worked; it was not hard for him to engrave the diploma in his mind and develop it there. I do not know how long he continued this imaging, but it must have been for some months.

Results followed as he persisted. One of the doctors took a great liking to this young boy, and after training him in the art of sterilizing instruments, giving hypodermic injections, along with other miscellaneous first aid work, he became a technical assistant in his office. The doctor sent him to high school as also to college at his own expense.

Today this man is a prominent doctor in Montreal, Canada. He had a dream! A clear image in his mind! His wealth was in his mind.

Wealth is your idea, desire, talent, urge for service, capacity to give to mankind, your ability for usefulness to society, with your love for humanity in general.

This young boy operated a great law unconsciously. Troward says, 'Having seen the end, you have willed the means to the realization of the end.' The end in this boy's case was to be a physician. To imagine, see, and feel the reality of being a doctor now, to live with that idea, sustain it, nourish it, and to love it until through his imagination it penetrated the layers of the subconscious, became a conviction, and paved the way to the fulfilment of his dreams.

He could have said, 'I have no education.' 'I do not know the right people.' 'I am too old to go to school now.' 'I have no money; it would take years, and I am not intelligent.' He would then be beaten before he started. His wealth was in his use of the Spiritual Power within him which responded to his thought.

The means or the way in which our prayer is answered is always hidden from us, except that occasionally we may intuitively perceive a part of the process. "My ways are past finding out.' The ways are not known. The only thing a person has to do is to imagine—to accept the end in his mind, yet leave its realisation to the universal all pervasive subjective wisdom contained within.

Often the question is asked, "What should I do after meditating on the end- accepting my desire in consciousness? The answer is simple: You will be compelled to do whatever is necessary for the realisation of your ideal. The law of the subconscious is compulsion. The law of life is action and reaction. What we do is the automatic response to our inner movements of the mind, inner feeling, and conviction.

A few months ago as I went to sleep, I imagined I was reading one of my most popular books, *Magic of Faith*, in French. I began to realize that is, imagine this book going into all French-speaking nations. For several weeks I did this every night, falling asleep with the imaginary French edition of *Magic of Faith* in my hands.

Just before Christmas in 1954, I received a letter from a leading publisher in Paris, France, enclosing a contract drawn up, with a request just for my signature, giving him permission to publish and promote abroad the French edition of *Magic of Faith*, to all French-speaking countries.

You might ask me what did I do about the publishing of this book after prayer? I would have to say, 'Nothing! The subjective wisdom took over, and brought it to pass in its own way, which was a far better way than any method I could consciously devise.

All of our external movements, motions, and actions follow the inner movements of the mind. Inner action precedes all outer action. Whatever steps you take physically, or what you seem to do objectively will all be a part of a pattern which you were compelled to fulfil.

Accepting the end manages the means to the realization of the end. Believe that you have it now—you shall receive it.

We must cease denying our good. Realize that the only thing that keeps us from the riches that lie all around us is our mental attitude, or the way we look at God, life, indeed the world in general. Know, believe, and act on the positive assumption that there is no reason why you cannot have, be or do whatever you wish to accomplish through the great laws of God.

Your knowledge of how your mind works is your savior and redeemer. Thought and feeling are your destiny. You possess everything by right of consciousness. The consciousness of health produces health; the consciousness of wealth produces wealth. The world seems to deny or oppose what you pray for; your senses sometimes mock and laugh at you.

If you say to your friend that you are opening up a new business for yourself, he may proceed to give you all the reasons why you are bound to fail. If you are susceptible to his hypnotic spell, he may instil fear of failure in your mind. As you become aware of the spiritual power which is one and indivisible, which responds to your thought, you will reject the darkness and ignorance of the world. You will know that you possess all the equipment, power along with the knowledge to succeed.

To walk on the Royal Road to Riches, you must not place obstacles on the pathway of others; neither must you be jealous or envious of others. Actually, when you entertain these negative states of mind, you are hurting and injuring yourself, because you are thinking and feeling it. "The suggestion,' as Quimby said, "you give to another, you are giving to yourself. This is the reason that the law of the golden rule is a cosmic, Divine law.

I am sure you have heard men say, "That fellow has a racket.' 'He is a racketeer.' 'He is getting money dishonestly.' 'He is a faker.' 'I knew him when he had nothing.' 'He is crooked, a thief, and a swindler. If you analyze the man who talks like that, he is usually in want or suffering from some financial or physical illness. Perhaps his former college friends went up the ladder of success and excelled him; now he is bitter and envious of their progress. In many instances this is the cause of his downfall.

Thinking negatively of these classmates, or condemning their wealth, causes the wealth and prosperity he is praying for to vanish and flee away. He is condemning the things he is praying for. He is praying two ways. On the one hand he is saying, 'God is making me prosper.' In the next breath, silently or audibly, he is saying, 'I resent that fellow's wealth. Always make it a special point to bless the other person—rejoice in his prosperity and success. When you do, you bless as well as prosper yourself.

If you go into the bank, and you see your competitor across the street deposit twenty times more than you do, or you see him deposit ten thousand dollars, rejoice and be exceedingly glad to see God's abundance being manifested through one of his sons. You are then blessing and exalting what you are praying for. What you bless, you multiply. What you condemn, you lose.

If you are working in a large organization, where you are silently thinking and resenting the fact that you are underpaid, that you are not appreciated, or that you deserve more money and greater recognition, you are subconsciously severing your ties with that organization. You are setting a law in motion; then the superintendent or manager says to you, "We have to let you go. You dismissed yourself. The manager was simply the instrument through which your own negative mental state was confirmed. In other words, he was a messenger telling you what you conceived as true about yourself. It was an example of the law of action and reaction. The action was the internal movement of your mind; the reaction was the response of the outer world to conform to your inner thinking.

Perhaps as you read this, you are thinking of someone who has prospered financially by taking advantage of others, by defrauding them, by selling them unsound investments in property, etc.

The answer to this is obvious, because if we rob, cheat, or defraud another, we do the same to ourselves. In reality, in this case we are actually hurting or robbing from ourselves. We are in a mood of lack in the first place, which is bound to attract loss to us. The loss may come in many ways; it may come in loss of health, prestige, peace of mind, social status, sickness in the home, or in business. It may not necessarily come in loss of money. We must not be shortsighted and think that the loss has to come in just dollars and cents.

Isn't it a wonderful feeling to place your head on the pillow at night, and feel you are at peace with the whole world, and that your heart is full of goodwill toward all? There are some people who have accumulated money the wrong way, by trampling on others, trickery, deceit, and chicanery. What is the price? Sometimes it is mental and physical disease, guilt complexes, insomnia, or hidden fears. As one man said to me, 'Yes, I rode roughshod over others. I got what I wanted, but I got cancer doing it.' He realized he had attained his wealth in the wrong way.

You can be wealthy and prosperous without hurting anyone. Many men are constantly robbing themselves; they steal from themselves: peace of mind, health, joy, inspiration, happiness, and the laughter of God. They may say that they have never stolen, but is it true? Every time we resent another, or are jealous, or envious of another's wealth or success, we are stealing from ourselves. These are the thieves and robbers which Jesus cast out of the temple; likewise, you must cast them out incisively and decisively. Do not let them live in your mind. Cut their heads off with the fire of right thought and feeling.

I remember in the early days of the war reading about a woman in Brooklyn, New York, who went around from store to store buying up all the coffee she could. She knew it was going to be rationed; she was full of fear that there would not be enough for her. She bought as much as she could, then stored it in the cellar. That evening she went to church services. When she came home, burglars had broken down the door, stolen not only the coffee, but silverware, money, jewellery, and other things.

This good woman said what they all say, 'Why did this happen to me when I was at church? I never stole from anyone.'

Is it true? Was she not in the consciousness of fear when she began to hoard supplies of coffee? Her mood of fear were sufficient to bring about loss in her home and possessions. She did not have to put her hand on the cash register or rob a bank; her fear of lack produced lack. This is the reason that many people who are what society calls, "Good citizens,' suffer loss. They are good in the worldly sense; i.e., they pay their taxes; they obey the laws, vote regularly, also are generous to charities, but they are resentful of others' possessions, their wealth, or social position. If they would like to take money when no one was looking, such an attitude is definitely and positively a state of shortage that may cause the person who indulges in such a mental state to attract charlatans or knaves who may swindle or cheat them in some business transaction.

Before the outer thief robs us, we have first robbed ourselves. There must be an inner thief, before the outer one appears.

A man can have a guilt complex, or accuse himself constantly. I knew such a man; he was very honest as a teller in a bank. He never stole any money, but he had an illicit romance; he was supporting another woman, and denying his family. He lived in fear that he would be discovered; a deep sense of guilt resulted. Fear follows guilt. Fear causes a contraction of the muscles and mucus membranes; acute sinusitis developed. Medication gave him only temporary relief.

I explained to this client the cause of his trouble. Simply, I told him the cure was to give up his outside affair. He said he couldn't; she was his soul mate—that he had tried. He was always condemning as well as accusing himself.

One day he was accused by one of the officials of the bank of having embezzled some money; it looked serious for him, as the evidence was circumstantial. He became panic-stricken as he realized the only reason he was wrongfully accused was that he had been accusing and condemning himself. He saw how mind operates.

Inasmuch as he was always accusing himself on the inner plane, he would be accused in his outside existence.

He immediately broke off the relationship with the other woman due to the shock of being accused of embezzling, and began to pray for Divine harmony and understanding between himself and the bank official. He began to claim, "There is nothing hidden that is not revealed. The peace of God reigns supreme in the minds and hearts of all concerned.'

Truth prevailed. The whole matter was dissolved in the light of truth. Another young man was discovered as the culprit. The bank teller knew that only through prayer was he saved from a jail sentence.

The great law is, 'As you would that men should think about you, think you about them in the same manner. As you would that men should feel about you, feel you also about them in like manner.'

Say from your heart, 'I wish for every man who walks the earth, what I wish for myself. The sincere wish of my heart is, therefore, peace, love, joy, abundance, and God's blessings to all men everywhere.' Rejoice and be glad in the progression, advancement, and prosperity of all men. Whatever you claim as true for yourself, claim it for all men everywhere. If you pray for happiness and peace of mind, let your claim be peace and happiness for all. Do not your organization, be glad.

Congratulate him, rejoice in his advancement as well as recognition. If you are angry or resentful, you are demoting yourself. Do not try to withhold from another his God- given birthright to all good things happiness, success, achievement, abundance, and Jesus said, "Store up for yourselves treasures in heaven, where the moth and the rust doth not consume, and where thieves cannot break through and steal.' Hatred and resentment rot to corrode the heart, causing us to become full of scars, impurities, toxins, and poisons.

The treasures of heaven are the truths of God—which we possess in our soul. Fill your minds with peace, harmony, faith, joy, honesty, integrity, loving kindness, and gentleness; then you will be sowing for yourself treasures in the heavens of your own mind.

If you are seeking wisdom regarding investments, or if you are worried about your stocks or bonds, quietly claim, 'Infinite Intelligence governs and watches over all my financial transactions, whatsoever I do shall prosper.' Do this frequently, you will find that your investments will be wise; moreover, you will be protected from loss, as you will be prompted to sell your securities or holdings before any loss accrues to you.

Use the following prayer daily regarding your home, business, and possessions: "'The overshadowing Presence which guides the planets on their course and causes the sun to shine, watches over all my possessions, home, business, and all my things.

God is my fortress and vault. All my possessions are secure in God. It is wonderful.' By reminding yourself daily of this great truth, as also by observing the laws of Love, you will always be guided, watched over, and prospered in all your ways. You will never suffer from loss, for you have chosen the Most High as your Counsellor and Guide. The envelope of God's Love surrounds, enfolds, to encompass you at all times. You rest in the Everlasting Arms of God.

All of us should seek an inner guidance for our problems. If you have a financial problem, repeat this before you retire at night: 'Now I shall sleep in peace. I have turned this matter over to the God-Wisdom within. It only knows the answer. As the sun rises in the morning, so will my answer be resurrected. I know the sunrise never fails.' Then go off to sleep.

Do not fret, fuss or fume over a problem. Night brings counsel. Sleep on it. Your intellect cannot solve all your problems. Pray for the Light that is to come. Remember that the dawn always comes; then the shadows flee away. Let your sleep every night be a contented bliss.

You are not a victim of circumstances, except if you believe you are. You can rise to overcome any circumstance or condition. You will have different experiences as you stand on the rock of spiritual Truth, steadfast, and faithful to your deeper purposes as well as desires.

In large stores, the management employs store detectives to prevent people from stealing; they catch a number every day trying to get something for nothing. All such people are living in the consciousness of lack and limitation.

They are stealing from themselves, attracting at the same time all manner of loss. These people lack faith in God, the without the understanding of how their minds work. If they would pray for true place, Divine expression, and supply, they would find work; then by honesty, integrity, and perseverence they would become a credit to themselves and society at large.

Jesus said, 'For ye have the poor always with you; but me ye have not always. The poor states of consciousness are always with us in this sense, that no matter how much wealth you now have, there is something you want with all your heart. It may be a problem of health; perhaps a son or daughter needs guidance, or harmony is lacking in the home. At that moment you are poor.

We could not know what abundance was, except we were conscious of lack. 'I have chosen twelve, and one you of is a devil.'

Whether it be the king of England or the boy in the slums, we are all born into limitation racial beliefs. It is through these limitations we grow. We could never discover the Inner Power, except through problems and difficulties; these are our poor states, which prod us in seeking the solution. We could not know what joy was, except when we could shed a tear of sorrow. We must be aware of poverty, to seek liberation and freedom: to ascend into God's opulence.

The poor states, such as fear, ignorance, worry, lack, and pain, are not bad when they cause you to seek the opposite. When you get into trouble, and get kicked from pillar to post; when you ask negative, heart-rending questions, such as 'Why are all these things happening to me? Why does there seem to be a jinx following me? — light will come into your mind. Through your suffering, pain, or misery you will discover the truth, which sets you free. Sweet are the uses of adversity, like a toad ugly and venomous, yet wears a precious jewel on its head.'

Through dissatisfaction we are led to satisfaction. All those studying the laws of life have been dissatisfied with something. They have had some problem or difficulty which they could not solve; or they were not satisfied with the man-made answers to life's riddles. They have found their answer in the God-Presence within themselves—the pearl of great price—the precious jewel. The Bible says, "I sought the Lord, and I found him, and He delivered me from all my fears.'

When you realize your ambition or desire, you will be satisfied for only a brief period of time; then the urge to expand will come again. This is Life seeking to express Itself at higher levels through you. When one desire is satisfied, another comes, etc. until infinity. You are here to grow. Life is progression; it is not static. You are here to go from glory to glory: there is no end; for there is no end to God's glory.

We are all poor in the sense we are forever seeking more light, wisdom, happiness, to gain greater joy out of life. God is Infinite. Never in Eternity could you exhaust the glory, beauty, and wisdom which is within; this is how wonderful you are.

In the absolute state all things are finished, but in the relative world we must awaken to that glory, which was ours before this world. No matter how wise you are, you are seeking more wisdom; so you are still poor. No matter how intelligent you are in the field of mathematics, physics, or astronomy, you are only scratching the surface. You are still poor. The journey is ever onward, upward, and Godward.

It is really an awakening process, whereby you realize creation is finished. When you know God does not have to learn, grow, expand, or unfold, you begin to gradually awaken from the dream of limitation, to become alive in God. As the scales of fear, ignorance, race belief, and mass hypnosis fall from your eyes, you begin to see as God sees. The blind spots are removed; then you begin to see the world as God made it; for we begin to see it through God's eyes. Now you say, 'Behold, the Kingdom of Heaven is at hand!

Feed the 'poor' within you; clothe the naked ideas, to give them form by believing in the reality of the idea, trusting the great Fabricator within to clothe it in form to make it a .material fact. Now your word (idea) shall become flesh (take form). When you are hungry (poor states), you seek food. When worried, you seek peace. When you are sick, you seek health; when you are weak, you seek strength. Your desire for prosperity is the voice of God in you telling you that abundance is yours; therefore, through your poor state, you find the urge to grow, to expand, to unfold, to achieve, and to accomplish your desires.

A pain in your shoulder is a blessing in disguise; it tells you to do something about it at once. If there were no pain and no indication of trouble, your arm might fall off on the street.

Your pain is God's alarm system telling you to seek His Peace and His Healing Power, to move from darkness to Light. When cold, you build a fire. When you are hungry, you eat. When you are in lack, enter into the mood of opulence and plenty. Imagine the end; rejoice in it. Having imagined the end, and felt it as true, you have willed the means to the realization of the end.

When you are fearful and worried, feed your mind with the great truths of God that have stood the test of time and will last forever. You can receive comfort by meditating on the great Psalms. For example: "'The Lord is my shepherd; I shall not want.' 'God is my refuge, my salvation, whom shall I fear? 'God is an ever-present help in time of trouble.' 'My God; in Him will I trust.' 'He shall cover me with His feathers, and under His wings shall I rest.' 'One with God is a majority.' 'If God be for me, who can be against me?' 'I do all things through Christ, who strengthened me'- eneth me.' Let the healing vibrations of these truths flood your mind and heart; then you will crowd out of your mind all your fears, doubts, and worries through this meditative process.

Imbibe another great spiritual truth: 'A merry heart maketh a cheerful countenance.' 'A merry heart hath a continual feast.' A merry heart doeth good like a medicine; a broken spirit drieth the bones.'

'Therefore I put thee in remembrance that thou stir up the gift of God within thee.' Begin now to stir up the gift of God by completely rejecting the evidence of senses, the tyranny and despotism of the race mind, to give complete recognition to the spiritual Power within you as the only Cause, the only Power, and the only Presence. Know that it is a responsive and beneficent Power. 'Draw nigh unto it, and it will draw nigh unto you.' Turn to It devotedly with assurance, trust, and love; it will respond to you as love, peace, guidance, and prosperity.

It will be your Comforter, Guide, Counsellor, and your heavenly Father. You will then say, 'God is Love. I have found Him. He truly has delivered me from all my fears.' Further-more, you will find yourself in green pastures, where abundance—all of God's riches flow freely through you.

Say to yourself freely and joyously during the day, 'I walk in the consciousness of the Presence of God all day long.' 'His fullness flows through me at all times, filling up all the empty vessels in my life.'

When you are filled to the brim of the feeling of being what you long to be, your prayer is answered. Are all the vessels full in your life? Look under health, wealth, love, and expression. Are you fully satisfied on all levels? Is there something lacking in one of these four? All that you seek, no matter what it is, comes under one of these classifications.

If you say, 'All I want is truth or wisdom, you are expressing the desire of all men everywhere. That is what everyone wants, even though he or she may word it differently. Truth or wisdom is the over-all desire of every man; this comes under the classification of expression. You wish to express more and more of God here, just now.

Through your emptiness, limitation, and problems, you grow in God's Light, to you discover yourself. There is no other way you could discover yourself.

If you could not use your powers two ways, you would never discover yourself; neither would you ever deduce a law governing you. If you were compelled to be good, or compelled to love, that would not be love. You would then be an automaton. You have freedom to love, because you can give it, or retain it. If compelled to love, there is no love. Aren't you flattered when some woman tells you she loves you and wants you? She has chosen you from all the men in the world. She does not have to love you. If she were forced to love you, you would not be flattered or happy about it.

You have freedom to be a murderer or a holy man. That is the reason that we praise such men as Lincoln and others. They decided to choose the good; we praise them for their choice.

If we believe that circumstances, conditions, events, age, race, religious training, or early environment can preclude the possibility of our attaining a happy, prosperous life, we are thieves and robbers. All that is necessary to express happiness and prosperity is to feel happy and prosperous. The feeling of wealth produces wealth. States of consciousness manifest themselves. This is why it is said, 'All that ever came before me (feeling) are thieves and robbers.' Feeling is the law, and the law is feeling.

Your desire for prosperity is really the promise of God saying that His riches are yours; accept this promise without any mental reservation.

Quimby likened prayer to a lawyer pleading the case before the judge. This teacher of the laws of mind said he could prove the defendant was not guilty as charged, but that the person was a victim of lies and false beliefs. You are the judge; you render your own verdict; then you are set free. The negative thoughts of want, poverty, and failure are all false; they are all lies; there is nothing to back them up.

You know there is only one spiritual Power, one primal cause, and you, therefore, cease giving power to conditions, circumstances, and opinions of men.

Give all Power to the Spiritual Power within you, knowing that It will respond to your thought of abundance and prosperity. Recognizing the supremacy of the Spirit within, and the Power of your own thought or mental image, is the way to opulence, freedom, and constant supply.

Accept the abundant life in your own mind. Your mental acceptance and expectancy of wealth has its own mathematics and mechanics of expression.

As you enter into the mood of opulence, all things necessary for the abundant life will come to pass. You are now the judge arriving at a decision in the courthouse of your mind.

You have, like Quimby, produced indisputable evidence showing how the laws of your mind work, and you are now free from fear. You have executed and chopped the heads off all the fear and superstitious thoughts in your mind. Fear is the signal for action; it is not really bad; it tells you to move to the opposite, which is faith in God and all positive values.

Let this be your daily prayer; write it in your heart: 'God is the source of my supply. That supply is my supply now. His riches flow to me freely, copiously, and abundantly. I am forever conscious of my true worth. I give of my talents freely, and I am wonderfully, divinely compensated. Thank you, Father!'

The Road to Riches

Riches are of the mind. Let us suppose for a moment that a physician's diploma was stolen together with his office equipment. I am sure you would agree that his wealth was in his mind. He could still carry on, diagnose disease, prescribe, operate, and lecture on materia medica. Only his symbols were stolen; he could always get additional supplies. His riches were in his mental capacity, knowledge to help others, and his ability to contribute to humanity in general.

You will always be wealthy when you have an intense desire to contribute to the good of mankind. Your urge for service—i.e., to give of your talents to the world—will always find a response in the heart of the universe.

I knew a man in New York during the financial crisis of 1929, who lost everything he had, including his home and all his life's savings. I met him after a lecture which I had given at one of the hotels in the city. This was what he said: 'I lost everything. I made a million dollars in four years. I will make it again. All I have lost is a symbol. I can again attract the symbol of wealth in the same way that honey attracts flies.'

I followed the career of this man for several years to discover the key to his success. The key may seem strange to you; yet it is a very old one. The name he gave the key was, 'Change water into wine! He read this passage in the Bible, and he knew it was the answer to perfect health, happiness, peace of mind, and prosperity.

Wine in the Bible always means the realization of your desires, urges, plans, dreams, propositions, etc.; in other words, it is the things you wish to accomplish, achieve, and bring forth.

Water in the Bible usually refers to your mind or consciousness. Water takes the shape of any vessel into which it is poured; likewise, whatever you feel and believe as true will become manifest in your world; thus you are always changing water into wine.

The Bible was written by enlightened men; it teaches practical, everyday psychology and a way of life. One of the cardinal tenets of the Bible is that you determine, mould, fashion, and shape your own destiny through right thought, feeling, and beliefs. It teaches you that you can solve any problem, overcome any situation, and that you are born to succeed, to win, and to triumph. In order to discover the Royal Road to Riches, and receive the strength and security necessary to advance in life, you must cease viewing the Bible in the traditional way.

The above man while in a financial crisis used to say to himself frequently during the days when he was without funds, 'I can change water into wine! These words meant to him, 'I can exchange the poverty ideas in my mind for the realization of my present desires or needs which are wealth and financial supply."

His mental attitude (water) was, 'Once I made a fortune honestly. I will make it again (wine).' His regular affirmation consisted of, 'I attracted the symbol (money) once, I am attracting it again. I know this, and feel it is true (wine).'

This man went to work as a salesman for a chemical organization. Ideas for the better promotion of their products came to him; he passed them on to his organization. It was not long until he became vice president. Within four years the company made him president. His constant mental attitude was, 'I can change water into wine!

Look upon the story in John of changing water into wine in a figurative way, and say to yourself as the above mentioned chemical salesman did: 'I can make the invisible ideas, urges, dreams, and desires of mine visible, because I have discovered a simple, universal law of mind.'

The law he demonstrated is the law of action and reaction. It means your external world, body, circumstances, environment, and financial status are always a perfect reflection of your inner thinking, beliefs, feelings, and convictions.

This being true, you can now change your inner pattern of thought by dwelling on the idea of success, wealth, and peace of mind. As you busy your mind with these latter concepts, these ideas will gradually seep into your mentality like seeds planted in the ground. As all seeds (thoughts and ideas) grow after their kind, so will your habitual thinking and feeling manifest in prosperity, success, and peace of mind. Wise thought (action) is followed by right action (reaction).

You can acquire riches when you become aware of the fact that prayer is a marriage feast. The feast is a psychological one; you meditate on (mentally eat of) your good or your desire until you become one with it.

I will now cite a case history from my files relating how a young girl performed her first miracle in transforming 'water into wine.' She operated a very beautiful hair salon. Her mother became ill, and she had to devote considerable time at home, neglecting her business. During her absence two of her assistants embezzled funds. She was forced into bankruptcy, lost her home, and found herself deeply in debt. She was unable to pay hospital bills for her mother, and she was now unemployed.

I explained to this woman the magic formula of changing water into wine.

Again we made it clear to her that wine means answered prayer or the materialisation of her ideal.

She was quarreling with the outside world. She said, 'Look at the facts: I have lost everything; it is a cruel world. I cannot pay my bills. I do not pray, for I have lost hope.' She was so absorbed and engrossed in the material world, that she was completely oblivious to the internal cause of her situation. As we talked, she began to understand that she had to resolve the quarrel in her mind.

No matter what your desire or ideal is as you read this book, you will also find some thought or idea in your mind opposed to it. For example, your desire may be for health; perhaps there are several thoughts such as these in your mind simultaneously: 'I can't be healed. I have tried, but it is no use; it's getting worse.' 'I don't know enough about spiritual mind healing.'

As you study yourself, don't you have a tug of war in your mind? Like this girl, you find environment and external affairs challenging your desire of expression, wealth, and peace of mind.

True prayer is a mental marriage feast, and it teaches us all how to resolve the mental conflict. In prayer, you 'write' what you believe in your own mind. Emerson said, 'A man is what he thinks all day long.

By your habitual thinking you make your own mental laws of belief. By repeating a certain train of thought you establish definite opinions and beliefs in the deeper mind called the subconscious; then such mental acceptances, beliefs, and opinions direct and control all the outer actions.

To understand this and begin to apply it is the first step in changing 'water into wine,' or changing lack and limitation into abundance and opulence. The man who is unaware of his own inner spiritual powers is, therefore, subject to race beliefs, lack, and limitation.

Open your Bible now, and perform your first miracle, as this beauty operator did. You can do it. If you merely read the Bible as a historical event, you will miss the spiritual, mental, scientific view of the laws of mind with which we are concerned in this book.

Let us take this passage: 'And the third day there was a marriage in Cana of Galilee; and the mother of Jesus was there.' Galilee means your mind or consciousness. Cana means your desire. The marriage is purely mental or the subjective embodiment of your desire. This whole beautiful drama of prayer is a psychological one in which all the characters are mental states, feelings, and ideas within you.

One of the meanings of Jesus is illumined reason. The mother of Jesus means the feeling, moods, or emotions which possess us.

'And both Jesus was called, and his disciples, to the marriage. Your disciples are your inner powers and faculties enabling you to realize your desires. 'And when they wanted wine, the mother of Jesus saith unto him, They have no wine.' Wine, as we have stated, represents the answered prayer or the manifestation of your desire and ideals in life. You can now see this is an everyday drama taking place in your own life.

When you wish to accomplish something as this girl did—namely, finding work, supply, and a way out of your problem-suggestions of lack come to you, such as, "There is no hope. All is lost. I can't accomplish it; it is hopeless. This is the voice from the outside world saying to you, "They have no wine,' or 'Look at the facts. This is your feeling of want, limitation, or bondage speaking.

How do you meet the challenge of circumstances and conditions?

By now you are getting acquainted with the laws of mind, which are as follows: 'As I think and feel inside, so is my outside world; i.e., my body, finances, environment, social position, and all phases of my external relationship to the world and man.' Your internal, mental movements and imagery govern, control, and direct the external plane in your life.

The Bible says, "As he thinketh in his heart, so is he.' The heart is a Chaldean word meaning the subconscious mind. In other words, your thought must reach subjective levels by engaging the power of your subliminal self.

Thought and feeling are your destiny. Thought charged with feeling and interest is always subjectified, and becomes manifest in your world. Prayer is a marriage of thought and feeling, or your idea and emotion; this is what the marriage feast relates.

Any idea or desire of the mind felt as true comes to pass, whether it is good, bad, or indifferent. Knowing the law now that what you imagine and feel in your mind, you will express, manifest, or experience in the outside, enables you to begin to discipline your mind.

When the suggestion of lack, fear, doubt, or despair (they have no wine) comes to your mind, immediately reject it mentally by focusing your attention at once on the answered prayer, or the fulfillment of your desire.

The statements given in the Bible from John 2, 'Mine hour is not yet come,' and, 'Woman, what have I to do with thee,' are figurative, idiomatic, Oriental expressions.

As we paraphrase these quotations, woman means the negative feeling that you indulge in. These negative suggestions have no power or reality, because there is nothing to back them up.

A suggestion of lack has no power; the power is resident in your own thought and feeling.

What does God mean to you? God is the Name given to the One Spiritual

Power. God is the One Invisible Source from Which all things flow.

When your thoughts are constructive and harmonious, the Spiritual Power, being responsive to your thought flows as harmony, health, and abundance. Practice the wonderful discipline of completely rejecting every thought of want by immediately recognizing the availability of the Spiritual Power. Its response to your constructive thoughts and imagery; then you will be practicing the truth found in these words, 'Woman, what have I to do with thee?'

We read, 'Mine hour is not yet come. This means that while you have not yet reached a conviction or positive state of mind, you know you are on the way mentally, because you are engaging your mind on the positive ideals, goals, as well as enhancing your objectives of life. Whatever the mind dwells upon, it multiplies, magnifies, and causes it to grow until finally the mind becomes qualified with the new state of consciousness. You are then conditioned positively, whereas before you were conditioned negatively.

The spiritual man in prayer moves from the mood of want to the mood of confidence, peace, and trust in the Spiritual Power within himself. Since his trust and faith are in the Spiritual Power, his mother (moods and feeling) registers a feeling of triumph or victory; this will bring about the solution or the answer to your prayer.

The water pots in the story from the Bible refer to the mental cycles that man goes through in order to bring about the subjective realization of his desire. The length of time may be a moment, hour, week, or month, depending on the faith and state of consciousness of the student.

In prayer we must cleanse our mind of false beliefs, fear, doubt, and anxiety by becoming completely detached from the evidence of senses—that is, the external world. In the peacefulness, quietude of your mind, when you have stilled the wheels of your mind, meditate on the joy of the answered prayer until that inner certitude comes. Indeed, you know that you know. When you have succeeded in being one with your desire, you have succeeded in the mental marriage—or the union of your feelings with your idea.

I am sure you wish to be married (one with) to health, harmony, success, as also achievement in your mind at this moment. Every time you pray you are trying to perform the marriage feast of Cana (realization of your desire or ideals). You want to be mentally identified with the concepts of peace, success, well-being, and perfect health.

"They filled them up to the brim.' The six waterpots represent your own mind in spiritual as well as mental creative activity. You must fill your mind to the brim, meaning you must become fulfilled. When you succeed in filling your mind with the ideal you wish to accomplish or express, you are full to the brim; then you cease praying about it; for you feel its reality in your mind. You know! It is a finished state of consciousness. You are at peace about it.

'And he saith unto them Draw out now, and bear unto the governor of the feast. Whatever is impregnated in our subconscious mind is always objectified on the screen of space; consequently, when we enter a state of conviction that our prayer is answered, we have given the command, 'Bear unto the governor of the feast.'

You are always governing your mental feast. During the day thousands of thoughts, suggestions, opinions, sights, and sounds reach your eyes and ears. You can reject them as unfit for mental consumption or entertain them, as you choose.

Your conscious, reasoning, intellectual mind is the governor of the feast. When you consciously choose to entertain, meditate, feast upon, and imagine your heart's desire as true, it becomes a living embodiment and a part of your mentality, so that your deeper self gives birth or expression to it.

In other words, what is impressed subjectively is expressed objectively. Your senses or conscious mind see the materization of your good attitude. When the conscious mind becomes aware of 'water made into wine,' it becomes aware of the answered prayer. Water might be called, also, the invisible, formless, spiritual power, unconditioned consciousness. Wine is conditioned consciousness, or the mind giving birth to its beliefs as well as convictions.

The servants which draw the water for you represent the mood of peace, confidence, and faith. According to your faith or feeling, your good is attracted or drawn to you.

Imbibe, cherish, fall in love with these spiritual principles which are discussed in this book. In the first recorded miracle of Jesus, you are told that prayer is a marriage feast, or the mind uniting with its desire.

Love is the fulfilling of the law. Love is really an emotional attachment, a sense of oneness with your good. You must be true to that which you love. You must be loyal to your purpose or to your ideal.

We are not being true to the one we love when we are flirting or mentally entertaining other marriages with fear, doubt, worry, anxiety, or false beliefs. Love is a state of oneness, a state of fulfillment. (Refer to the book by the author, Love is Freedom.)

When this simple drama was explained to the beauty operator mentioned above, she became rich mentally. She understood this drama. She put it into practice in her life. This is how she prayed: She knew that the water (her own mind) would flow, to fill up all the empty vessels in response to her new way of thinking and feeling.

At night this client became very quiet and still, relaxed her body, to begin to use constructive imagery. The steps she used are as follows:

First step: She began to imagine the local bank manager was congratulating her on her wonderful deposits in the bank. She kept imagining that for about five minutes.

The second step: In her imagination she heard her mother saying to her, 'I am so happy about your wonderful, new position. She continued to hear her say this in a happy, joyous way for about three to five minutes.

The third step: She vividly imagined the writer was in front of her performing her marriage ceremony. This woman heard me saying as the officiating minister, 'I now pronounce you man and wife. Completing this routine, she went to sleep feeling filled full, i.e., sensing and feeling within herself the joy of the answered prayer.

Nothing happened for three weeks; in fact, things got much worse, but she persevered, refusing to take, "No,' for her answer. She knew that in order to grow spiritually, she, too, had to perform her first miracle by changing her fear to faith, her mood of lack to a mood of opulence and prosperity, by changing consciousness (water) into the conditions, circumstances, and experiences she wished to express.

Consciousness, Awareness, Beingness, Principle, Spirit, or whatever Name you give It, is the cause of all; It is the only Presence and Power. The Spiritual Power or Spirit within us is the cause and substance of all things. All things, birds, trees, stars, sun, moon, earth, gold, silver, and platinum-are its manifestations. It is the cause and substance of all things. "There is none else.'

Understanding this, she knew that water (consciousness) could become supply in the form of money, true place, or true expression for herself, health for her mother, as well as companionship and fullness of life. She saw this simple yet profound—truth in the twinkling of an eye, as she said to me, 'I accept my good.

She knew that nothing is hidden from us; all of God is within us, waiting for our discovery and inquiry.

In less than a month this young girl got married. The writer performed the ceremony. I pronounced the words she heard me say over and over again in her meditative, relaxed state, I now pronounce you man and wife!

Her husband gave her a check for $24,000 as a wedding present, as well as a trip around the world. Her new expression as a beauty operator was to beautify her home and garden, to make the desert of her mind rejoice and blossom as the rose.

She changed 'water into wine.' Water or her consciousness became charged or conditioned by her constant, true, happy imagery. These images, when sustained regularly, systematically, along with faith in the developing powers of the deeper mind, will come out of the darkness (subconscious mind) into light (objectified on the screen of space).

There is one important rule: Do not expose this newly developed film to the shattering light of fear, doubt, despondency,or worry. Whenever worry or fear knocks at your door, immediately turn to the picture you developed in your mind, as you say to yourself, 'A beautiful picture is being developed now in the dark house of my mind.' Mentally pour on that picture your feeling of joy, faith, and understanding. You know you have operated a psychological, spiritual law; for what is impressed shall be expressed. It is wonderful!

The following is a sure, certain way for developing as also manifesting all the material riches—supply, you need all the days of your life.

If you apply this formula sincerely with true honesty, you should be amply rewarded on the external plane. I will illustrate this by telling you of a man who came to see me in London in desperate, financial straits. He was a member of the Church of England, who had studied the working of the subconscious mind to some extent.

I told him to say frequently during the day, 'God is the source of my supply.

All my needs are met at every moment of time and point of space.' Think also of all the animal life in this world, of all the galaxies of space which are now being taken care of by an Infinite Intelligence. Notice how nature is lavish, extravagant, and bountiful. Think of the fish of the sea which are all being sustained, as well as the 'birds of the air!

He began to realize that since he was born, he had been taken care of, fed by his mother, clothed by his father, that is watched over by tender, loving parents.

This man got a job and was paid in a wonderful way. He reasoned that it was illogical to assume that the Principle of Life, which gave him life—always took care of him, would suddenly cease to respond to him.

He realized that he had cut off his own supply by resenting his employer, self- condemnation, criticism of himself, and by his own sense of unworthiness. He had psychologically severed the cord which joined him to the Infinite Source of all things—the Indwelling Spirit or Life Principle, called by some, 'Consciousness or Awareness.'

Man is not fed like the birds; he must consciously commune with the Inner dwelling Power and Presence, to receive guidance, strength, vitality that is all things necessary for the fulfillment of his needs.

This is the formula which he used to change water into the wine of abundance to achieve financial success. He realized God or the Spiritual Power within him was the cause of all; furthermore, he realized that if he could sell himself the idea that wealth was his by Divine right, he would manifest abundance of supply.

The affirmation he used was, 'God is the source of my supply. All my financial and other needs are met at every moment of time and point of space; there is always a Divine surplus.' This simple statement repeated frequently, knowingly, with intelligent conviction, conditioned his mind to a prosperity consciousness.

All he had to do was to sell himself this positive idea, in the same way a good salesman has to sell the merits of his product. Such a person is convinced of the integrity of his company, the high quality of the product, the good service which it will give the customer, and the fact that the price is right, etc.

I told him whenever negative thoughts came to his mind, which would happen, not to fight or quarrel with them in any way, but simply go back to the spiritual, mental formula, and repeat it quietly and lovingly to himself. Negative thoughts came to him in avalanches at times, in the form of a flood of negativity. Each time he met them with the positive, firm, loyal conviction: 'God supplies all my needs; there is a Divine surplus in my life.'

He said that as he drove his car, went through his day's routine, a host of sundry, miscellaneous, negative concepts crowded his mind from time to time, such as "'There is no hope.' 'You are broke.'

Each time such negative thoughts came, he refused their mental admission by turning to the Eternal Source of wealth, health—all things which he knew to be his own spiritual awareness.

Definitely, most positively he claimed, "God is the source of my supply, and that supply is mine now! Or," There is a Divine solution.

God's wealth is my wealth,' with other affirmative, positive statements, which charged his mind with hope, faith, expectancy.

Ultimately this conviction in an everflowing fountain of riches, supplyed all his needs copiously, joyously—endlessly.

The negative flood of thoughts came to him as often as fifty times in an hour; each time he refused to open the door of his mind to these gangsters, assassins, and thieves, which he knew would only rob him of peace, wealth, success,—all good things.

Instead he opened the door of his mind to the idea of God's Eternal Life Principle of supply flowing through him as wealth, health, energy, power, and all things necessary to lead a full and happy life here.

As he continued to do this, the second day not so many thieves knocked at his door; the third day, the flow of negative visitors was less; the fourth day, they came intermittently, hoping for admission, but receiving the same mental response: 'No entrance! I accept only thoughts or concepts, which activate, heal, bless, to inspire my mind!

He reconditioned his consciousness or mind to a wealth consciousness. "The prince of this world cometh, and hath nothing in me. This conveys to your mind: The negative thoughts, such as fear, lack, worry, anxiety, came, but they received no response from his mind. He was now immune, God-intoxicated, seized by a divine faith in an ever-expanding consciousness of abundance and financial supply.

This man did not lose everything; neither did he go into bankruptcy. He was given extended credit; his business improved; new doors opened up: he prospered.

Remember always in the prayer-process, you must be loyal to your ideal, purpose, and objective. Many people fail to realize wealth and financial success, because they pray two ways.

They affirm God is their supply, and that they are Divinely prospered, but a few minutes later they deny their good by saying, 'I can't pay this bill.' 'I can't afford this, that, or the other thing.

Or they say to themselves, 'A jinx is following me.' 'I can't ever make ends meet.' 'I never have enough to go around.' All such statements are highly destructive and neutralize your positive prayers. This is what is called 'praying two ways.'

You must be faithful to your plan or your goal. You must be true to your knowledge of the Spiritual Power. Cease making negative marriages, i.e., uniting with negative thoughts, fears, and worries.

Prayer is like a captain directing the course of his ship. You must have a destination. You must know where you are going. The captain of the ship, knowing the laws of navigation, regulates his course accordingly. If the ship is turned from its course by storms or unruly waves, he calmly redirects it along its true course. You are the captain on the bridge, and you are giving the orders in the way of thoughts, feelings, opinions, beliefs, moods, and mental tones. Keep your eye on the beam.

You go where your vision is! Cease, therefore, looking at all the obstacles, delays, and impediments that would cause you to go off your course.

Be definite and positive. Decide where you are going. Know that your mental attitude is the ship which will take you from the mood of lack and limitation, to the mood and feeling of opulence, and to the belief in the inevitable law of God working for you.

Quimby, who was a doctor, a wonderful student, and teacher of the mental and spiritual laws of mind, said, 'Man acts as he is acted upon.

What moves you now? What is it that determines your response to life? The answer is as follows: Your ideas, beliefs, and opinions activate your mind and condition you to the point that you become, as Quimby stated, "An expression of your beliefs.' This illustrates the truth of Quimby's statement: 'Man is belief expressed.'

Another popular statement of Quimby's was, "Our minds mingle like atmospheres, and each person has his identity in that atmosphere.

When you were a child, you were subject to the moods, feelings, beliefs, and the general mental atmosphere of the home. The fears, anxieties, superstitions, as well as the religious faith and convictions of the parents were impressed on your mind.

Let us say the child had been brought up in a povertystricken home, in which there was never enough to go 8 Augaround, financially speaking; he heard constantly the complaint of lack and limitation.

You could say, like Salter in his conditioned reflex therapy, that the child was conditioned to poverty. The young man may have a poverty complex based on his early experiences, training, and beliefs, but he can rise above any situation and become free; this is done through the power of prayer.

I knew a young boy, aged 17, who was born in a place called, 'Hell's Kitchen,' in New York. He listened to some lectures I was giving in Stein-way Hall, New York, at the time.

This boy realized that he had been the victim of negative, destructive thinking, and that if he did not redirect his mind along constructive channels, the world-mind with its fears, failures, hates, and jealousies would move in and control him. 'Man acts as he is acted upon.'

It stands to reason, as Quimby knew, that if man will not take charge of his own house (mind), the propaganda, false beliefs, fears, and worries of the phenomenalistic world will act as a hypnotic spell over him.

We are immersed in the race mind which believes in sickness, death, misfortune, accident, failures, disease, and diverse disasters. Follow the Biblical injunction: 'Come out from among them, and be separate.' Identify yourself mentally and emotionally with the Eternal Verities which have stood the test of time.

This young man decided to think and plan for himself. He decided to take the Royal Road to Riches by accepting God's abundance here and now, and to fill his mind with spiritual concepts and perceptions.

He knew, as he did this, he would automatically crowd out of his mind all negative patterns.

He adopted a simple process called, 'scientific imagination. He had a wonderful voice, but it was not cultivated or developed.

I told him the image he gave attention to in his mind would be developed in his deeper mind and come to pass. He understood this to be a law of mind—a law of action and reaction—i.e., the response of the deeper mind to the mental picture held in the conscious mind.

This young man would sit down quietly in his room at home, relax his whole body, and vividly imagine himself singing before a microphone.

He would actually reach out for the 'feel of the instrument. He would hear me congratulate him on his wonderful contract and tell him how magnificent his voice was.

By giving his attention and devotion to this mental image regularly and systematically, a deep impression was made on his subconscious mind.

A short time elapsed, and an Italian voice instructor in New York gave him free lessons several times a week, because he saw his possibilities.

He got a contract which sent him abroad to sing in the salons of Europe, Asia, South Africa, and other places. His financial worries were over, for he also received a wonderful salary.

His hidden talents and ability to release them were his real riches. These talents and powers within all of us are God-given; let us release them.

Did you ever say to yourself, 'How can I be more useful to my fellow creatures?' 'How can I contribute more to humanity?'

A minister-friend of mine told me that in his early days he and his church suffered financially.

His technique or process was this simple prayer which worked wonders for him, 'God reveals to me better ways to present the truths of God to my fellow creatures.' Money poured in; the mortgage was paid in a few years, and he has never worried about money since.

As you read this chapter, you have now learned that the inner feelings, moods, and beliefs of man always control and govern his external world. The inner movements of the mind control the outer movements. To change the outside, you must change the inside. 'As in Heaven, so on earth;' or as in my mind or consciousness, so is it in my body, circumstances, and environment.

The Bible says, 'There is nothing hidden that shall not be revealed. For example, if you are sick, you are revealing a mental and emotional pattern which is the cause.

If you are upset, or if you receive tragic news, notice how you reveal it in your face, eyes, gestures, tonal qualities, also in your gait, and posture.

As a matter of fact, your whole body reveals your inner distress. You could, of course, through mental discipline and prayer remain absolutely poised, serene, and calm, refusing to betray your hidden feelings or mental states. You could order the muscles of your body to relax, be quiet, and be still; they would have to obey you.

Your eyes, face, and lips would not betray any sign of grief, anger, or despondency. On the other hand, with a little discipline, through prayer and meditation, you could reverse the entire picture. Even though you had received disturbing news, regardless of its grave nature, you could show and exhibit joy, peace, relaxation, and a vibrant, buoyant nature.

No one would ever know that you were the recipient of so-called bad news.

Regardless of what kind of news you received today, you could go to the mirror, look at your face, lips, eyes, and your gestures, as you tell yourself and imagine you have heard the news of having received a vast fortune. Dramatize it, feel it, thrill to it, and notice how your whole body responds to the inner thrill.

You can reverse any situation through prayer. Busy your mind with the concepts of peace, success, wealth, and happiness. Identify yourself with these ideas mentally, emotionally, and pictorially.

Get a picture of yourself as you want to be; retain that image; sustain it with joy, faith, and expectancy; finally you will succeed in experiencing its manifestation.

I say to people who consult me regarding financial lack to 'marry wealth.'

Some see the point; others do not. As all Bible students know, your wife is what you are mentally joined to, united with, or at one with.

In other words, what you conceive and believe, you give conception. If you believe the world is cold, cruel, and harsh, that it is a 'dog eat dog' way of life, that is your concept; you are married to it, and you will have children or issue by that marriage.

The children from such a mental marriage or belief will be your experiences, conditions, and circumstances, together with all other events in your life. All your experiences and reactions to life will be the image and likeness of the ideas which fathered them.

Look at the many wives the average man is living with, such as fear, doubt, anxiety, criticism, jealousy, and anger; these play havoc with his mind.

Marry wealth by claiming, feeling, and believing: 'God supplies all my needs according to his riches in glory.' Or take the following statement, and repeat it over and over again knowingly until your consciousness is conditioned by it, or it becomes part of your meditation: 'I am Divinely expressed, and I have a wonderful income.'

Do not say this in a parrot-like fashion, but know that your train of thought is being engraved in your deeper mind, and it becomes a conditioned state of consciousness. Let the phrase become meaningful to you. Pour life, love, and feeling on it, making it alive.

One of my class-students recently opened a restaurant. He phoned me, saying that he got married to a restaurant; he meant that he had made up his mind to be very successful, diligent, and persevering, and to see that his business prospered.

This man's wife (mental) was his belief in the accomplishment of his desire or wish.

Identify yourself with your aim in life, and cease mental marriages with criticism, self-condemnation, anger, fear, and worry. Give attention to your chosen ideal, being full of faith and confidence in the inevitable law of prosperity and success.

You will accomplish nothing by loving your ideal one minute, and denying it the next minute; this is like mixing acid and alkali, and you will get an inert substance. In going along the Royal Road to Riches, you must be faithful to your chosen ideal (your wife). We find illustrations in the Bible relating to these same truths. For instance, 'Eve came out of Adam's rib. Your rib is your concept, desire, idea, plan, goal, or aim in life.

Eve means the emotion, feeling nature, or the inner tone. In other words, you must mother the idea. The idea must be mothered, loved, and felt as true, in order to manifest your aim in life.

The idea is the father; the emotion is the mother; this is the marriage feast which is always taking place in your mind.

Ouspensky spoke of the third element which entered in or was formed following the union of your desire and feeling. He called it the neutral element. We may call it 'peace' for God is Peace.

The Bible says, 'And the government shall be on his shoulders.' In other words, let Divine Wisdom be your guide. Let the subjective Wisdom within you lead, guide, and govern you in all your ways.

Turn over your request to this Indwelling Presence, knowing in your heart and soul that it will dissipate the anxiety, heal the wound, and restore your soul to equanimity and tranquility. Open your mind and heart, and say, 'God is my pilot.

He leads me. He prospers me. He is my counsellor.' Let your prayer be night and morning, 'I am a channel through which God's riches flow ceaselessly, copiously, and freely.' Write that prayer in your heart, inscribe it in your mind. Keep on the beam of God's glory!

The man who does not know the inner workings of his own mind is full of burdens, anxieties, and worries; he has not learned how to cast his burden on the Indwelling Presence and go free. The Zen monk was asked by his disciple, 'What is Truth?' He replied in a symbolic way by taking the bag off his back, and placing it on the ground. The disciple then asked him, "Master, how does it work?

The Zen monk, still silent, placed the bag on his back, and walked on down the road singing to himself. The bag is your burden, or your problem. You cast it on the subjective Wisdom which knows all, and has the 'know how of accomplishment. It knows only the answer.

Placing the bag again on his back means though I still have the problem, I now have mental rest and relief from the burden, because I have invoked the Divine Wisdom on my behalf; therefore, I sing the song of triumph, knowing that the answer to my prayer is on the way, and I sing for the joy that is set before me. It is wonderful.

'Every man at the beginning doth set forth good wine; and when men have well drunk, then that which is worse; but thou hast kept the good wine until now.' This is true of every man when he first enters a knowledge of the laws of the mind.

He sets out with high spirits and ambitions. He is the new broom which sweeps clean, and he is full of good intentions; oftentimes he forgets the Source of power. He does not remain faithful to the Principle within him, which is scientific and effectual, that would lift him out of his negative experiences and set him on the high road to freedom and peace of mind.

He begins to indulge mentally and emotionally with ideas and thoughts extraneous to his announced aim and goal. In other words, he is not faithful to his ideal or wife.

Know that the subjective or deeper self within you. will accept your request, and being the great fabricator, it will bring it to pass in its own way. All you do is release your request with faith and confidence, in the same way you would cast a seed on the ground, or mail a letter to a friend, knowing the answer would come.

Did you ever go between two great rocks and listen to the echo of your voice? This is the way the Life Principle within you answers.

You will hear the echo of your own voice. Your voice is your inner, mental movement of the mind—your inner, psychological journey where you feasted mentally on an idea until you were full; then you rested.

Knowing this law and how to use it, be sure you never become drunk with power, arrogance, pride, or conceit. Use the law to bless, heal, inspire, and lift up others, as well as yourself.

Man misuses the law by selfishly taking advantage of his fellow man; if you do, you hurt and attract loss to yourself.

Power, security, and riches are not to be obtained externally. They come from the treasure-house of eternity within. We should realize that the good wine is always present, for God is the Eternal Now. Regardless of present circumstances, you can prove your good is ever-present by detaching yourself mentally from the problem, going on the High Watch, and going about your Father's business.

To go on the High Watch is to envision your good, to dwell on the new concept of yourself, to become married to it, and sustain the happy mood by remaining faithful—full of faith every step of the way—knowing that the wine of joy, the answered prayer, is on the way.

"Now is the day of salvation." "The kingdom of heaven is at hand.' 'Thou hast kept the good wine until now.' You can—this moment—travel psychologically in your mind, and enter mentally through Divine imagination into any desired state. The wealth, health, or invention you wish to introduce are all invisible at first. Everything comes out of the Invisible.

You must subjectively possess riches, before you can objectively possess wealth. The feeling of wealth produces wealth; for wealth is a state of consciousness. A state of consciousness is what you think, feel, believe, and mentally give consent to.

A teacher in California receiving over five or six thousand dollars a year looked in a window at a beautiful ermine coat that was priced at $8,000. She said, 'It would take me years to save that amount of money. I could never afford it.

Oh, how I want it! She listened to our lectures on Sunday mornings. By ceasing to marry these negative concepts, she learned that she could have a coat, car, or anything she wished without hurting anybody on the face of the earth.

I told her to imagine she had the coat on, to feel its beautiful fur, and to get the feel of it on her. She began to use the power of her imagination prior to sleep at night.

She put the imaginary coat on her, fondled it, caressed it, like a child does with her doll. She continued to do this, and finally felt the thrill of it all.

She went to sleep every night wearing this imaginary coat and being so happy in possessing it. Three months went by, and nothing happened.

She was about to waiver, but she reminded herself that it is the sustained mood which demonstrates. 'He who perseveres to the end shall be saved.' The solution will come to the person who does not waver, but always goes about with the perfume of His Presence with him. The answer comes to the man who walks in the light that 'It is done!

You are always using the perfume of His Presence when you sustain the happy, joyous mood of expectancy, knowing your good is on the way. You saw it in the unseen, and you know you will see it in the seen.

The sequel to the teacher's drama of the mind is interesting.

One Sunday morning after our lecture, a man accidentally stepped on her toe, apologized profusely, asked her where she lived, and offered to drive her home. She accepted gladly.

Shortly after, he proposed marriage, gave her a beautiful diamond ring, and said to her, 'I saw the most wonderful coat; you would simply look radiant wearing it!

It was the coat she admired three months previously. (The salesman said over one hundred wealthy women looked at the coat, admired it immensely, but for some reason always selected another garment.)

Through your capacity to choose, imagine the reality of what you have selected, and through faith and perseverance, you can realize your goal in life. All the riches of heaven are here now within you, waiting to be released. Peace, joy, love, guidance, inspiration, goodwill, and abundance all exist now. All that is necessary in order to express God's riches is for you to leave the present now (your limitation), enter into the mental vision or picture, and in a happy, joyous mood become one with your ideal.

Having seen and felt your good in moments of high exaltation, you know that in a little while you shall see your ideal objectively as you walk through time and space. As within, so without. As above, so below. As in heaven só on earth. In other words, you will see your beliefs expressed. Man is belief expressed!

About Dr. Joseph Murphy

Joseph Murphy was born on May 20, 1898, in a small town in the County of Cork, Ireland. His father, Denis Murphy, was a deacon and professor at the National School of Ireland, a Jesuit facility. His mother, Ellen, née Connelly, was a housewife, who later gave birth to another son, John, and a daughter, Catherine.

Joseph was brought up in a strict Catholic household. His father was quite devout and, indeed, was one of the few lay professors who taught Jesuit seminarians. He had a broad knowledge of many subjects and developed in his son the desire to study and learn.

Ireland at that time was suffering from one of its many economic depressions, and many families were starving. Although Denis Murphy was steadily employed, his income was barely enough to sustain the family.

Young Joseph was enrolled in the National School and was a brilliant student. He was encouraged to study for the priesthood and was accepted as a Jesuit seminarian. However, by the time he reached his late teen years, he began to question the Catholic orthodoxy of the Jesuits, and he withdrew from the seminary. Since his goal was to explore new ideas and gain new experiences—a goal he could not pursue in Catholicdominated Ireland—he left his family to go to America.

He arrived at the Ellis Island Immigration Center with only $5 in his pocket.

His first project was to find a place to live. He was fortunate to locate a rooming house where he shared a room with a pharmacist who worked in local drugstore.

Joseph's knowledge of English was minimal, as Gaelic was spoken both in his home and at school, so like most Irish immigrants, Joseph worked as a day laborer, earning enough to keep fed and housed.

He and his roommate became good friends, and when a job opened up at the drugstore where his friend worked, he was hired to be an assistant to the pharmacist. He immediately enrolled in a school to study pharmacy. With his keen mind and desire to learn, it didn't take long before Joseph passed the qualification exams and became a full-fledged pharmacist. He now made enough money to rent his own apartment. After a few years, he purchased the drugstore, and for the next few years ran a successful business.

When the United States entered World War II, Joseph enlisted in the Army and was assigned to work as a pharmacist in the medical unit of the 88th Infantry Division. At that time, he renewed his interest in religion and began to read extensively about various religious beliefs. After his discharge from the Army, he chose not to return to his career in pharmacy. He traveled extensively, taking courses in several universities both in the United States and abroad.

From his studies, Joseph became enraptured by the various Asian religions and went to India to learn about them in depth. He studied all of the major religions from the time of their beginning. He extended these studies to the great philosophers from ancient times until the present.

Although he studied with some of the most intelligent and far-sighted professors, the one person who most influenced Joseph was Dr Thomas Troward, who was a judge as well as a philosopher, doctor, and professor. Judge Troward became Joseph's mentor. From him he not only learned philosophy, theology, and law, but also was introduced to mysticism and particularly, the Masonic order. He became an active member of this order and over the years rose in the Masonic ranks to the 32nd degree in the Scottish Rite.

Upon his return to the United States, Joseph chose to become a minister and bring his broad knowledge to the public. As his concept of Christianity was not traditional and indeed ran counter to most of the Christian denominations, he founded his own church in Los Angeles. He attracted a small number of congregants, but it did not take long for his message of optimism and hope rather than the 'sin and damnation' sermons of so many ministers to attract many men and women to his church.

Dr Joseph Murphy was a proponent of the New Thought movement. This movement was developed in the late 19th and early 20th centuries by many philosophers and deep thinkers who studied this phenomenon and preached, wrote, and practiced a new way of looking at life. By combining a metaphysical, spiritual, and pragmatic approach to the way we think and live, they uncovered the secret of attaining what we truly desire.

The proponents of the New Thought movement preached a new idea of life that brings out new methods and more perfected results, and we have the power to use it to enrich our lives. We can do all these things only as we have found the law and worked out the understanding of the law, which God seemed to have written in riddles in the past.

Of course, Dr Murphy wasn't the only minister to preach this positive message. Several churches, whose ministers and congregants were influenced by the New Thought movement, were founded and developed in the decades following World War II. The Church of Religious Science, the Unity Church, and similar places of worship preach philosophies similar to this.

Dr Murphy named his organization The Church of Divine Science. He often shared platforms, conducted joint programs with his similar-thinking colleagues, and trained other men and women to join their ministry.

Over the years, other churches joined with him in developing an organization called the Federation of Divine Science, which acts an umbrella for all Divine Science churches.

Each of the Divine Science church leaders continues to push for more education, and Dr Murphy was one of the leaders to support the creation of the Divine Science School in St. Louis, Missouri, to train new ministers and provide ongoing educational education for both ministers and congregants.

The annual meeting of the Divine Science ministers was a must to attend, and Dr Murphy was a featured speaker at them. He encouraged the participants to study and continue to learn, particularly about the importance of the subconscious mind.

Over the next few years, Murphy's local Church of Divine Science grew so large that his building was too small to hold them. He rented The Wilshire Ebell Theater, a former movie theater. His services were so well attended that even this venue could not always accommodate all who wished to attend. Classes conducted by Dr Murphy and his staff supplemented his Sunday services that were attended by 1,300 to 1,500 people. These were supplemented by seminars and lectures that were held most days and evenings. The church remained at the Wilshire Ebell Theater in Los Angeles until 1976, when it moved to a new location in Laguna Hills, California, near a retirement community.

To reach the vast numbers of people who wanted to hear his message, Dr Murphy created a weekly radio talk show, which eventually reached an audience of over a million listeners.

Many of his followers wanted more than just summaries. They suggested that he tape his lectures and radio programs. He was at first reluctant to do so, but agreed to experiment. His radio programs were recorded on extra-large 78 rpm discs, a common practice at that time. He had six cassettes made from one of these discs and placed them on the information table in the lobby of the Wilshire Ebell Theater. They sold out the first hour. This started a new venture. His tapes of his lecture explaining biblical texts, and providing meditations and prayers for his listeners were not only sold in his church, but in other churches, bookstores, and via the mail.

As the church grew, Dr Murphy added a staff of professional and administrative personnel to assist him in the many programs in which he was involved and in researching and preparing his first books. One of the most effective members of his staff was his administrative secretary, Dr Jean Wright. The working relationship developed into a romance, and they were married-a lifelong partnership that enriched both of their lives.

At this time (the 1950s), there were very few major publishers of spiritually inspired material. The Murphy's located some small publishers in the Los Angeles area, and with them produced a series of small books (often 30 to 50 pages printed in pamphlet form) that were sold, mostly in churches, from $1.50 to $3.00 per book. When the orders for these books increased to the point where they required second and third printings, major publishers recognized that there was a market for such books and added them to their catalogs.

Dr Murphy became well known outside of the Los Angeles area as a result of his books, tapes, and radio broadcasts and was invited to lecture all over the country. He did not limit his lectures to religious matters, but spoke on the historical values of life, the art of wholesome living, and on the teachings of great philosophers—both from the Western and Oriental cultures.

As Dr Murphy never learned to drive, he had to arrange for somebody to drive him to the various places where he was invited to lecture and other places in his very busy schedule. One of Jean's functions as his administrative secretary and later as his wife was to plan his assignments, arrange for trains or flights, airport pickups, hotel accommodations, and all the other details of the trips.

The Murphy's traveled frequently to many countries around the world. One of his favorite working vacations was to hold seminars on cruise ships. These trips were for a week or more and would take him to many countries around the world. One of Dr Murphy's most rewarding activities was speaking to the inmates at many prisons. Many ex-convicts wrote him over the years, telling him how his words had truly turned their lives around and inspired them to live spiritual and meaningful lives.

He toured the United States and many countries in Europe and Asia. In his lectures, he emphasized the importance of understanding the power of the subconscious mind and the life principles based on belief in the one God, the 'I AM.'

Dr Murphy's pamphlet-sized books were so popular that he began to expand them into more detailed and longer works. His wife gave us some insight into his manner and method of writing. She reported that he wrote his manuscripts on a tablet and pressed so hard on his pencil or pen that you could read the page by the imprint on the next page. He seemed to be in a trance while writing. His writing style was to remain in his office for four to six hours without disturbance until he stopped and said that was enough for the day. Each day was the same.

He never went back into the office again until the next morning to finish what he'd started. He took no food or drink while he was working, He was just alone with his thoughts and his huge library of books, to which he referred from time to time. His wife sheltered him from visitors and calls and kept things moving for church business and other activities.

Dr Murphy was always looking for a simple way to discuss the issues and to elaborate points that would explain in detail how it affects the individual. He chose some of his lectures to present on cassettes, records, or CDs, as the technologies developed and new methods entered the audio field.

His entire work of CDs and cassettes are tools that can be used for most problems that individuals encounter in life, and have been time-tested to accomplish the goals as intended. His basic theme is that the solution to problems lies within oneself. Outside elements cannot change one's thinking. That is, your mind is your own. To live a better life, it's your mind not outside circumstances, that you must change.

You create your own destiny. The power of change is in your mind, and by using the power of your subconscious mind, you can make those changes for the better.

Dr Murphy wrote more than 30 books. His most famous work, *The Power of the Unconscious Mind*, which was first published in 1963, became an immediate bestseller. It was acclaimed as one of the best self-help guides ever written. Millions of copies have been sold and continue to be sold all over the world.

Among some of his other best-selling books were Telepsychics—The Magic Power of Perfect Living, The Amazing Laws of Cosmic Mind, Secrets of the I- Ching, The Miracle of Mind Dynamics, Your Infinite Power to Be Rich, and The Cosmic Power Within You.

Dr Murphy died in December 1981, and his wife, Dr Jean Murphy, continued his ministry after his death. In a lecture she gave in 1986, quoting her late husband, she reiterated his philosophy:

I want to teach men and women of their Divine Origin, and the powers regnant within them. I want to inform that this power is within and that they are their own saviors and capable of achieving their own salvation. This is the message of the Bible and nine-tenths of our confusion today is due to wrongful, literal interpretation of the life-transforming truths offered in it.

I want to reach the majority, the man on the street, the woman overburdened with duty and suppression of her talents and abilities. I want to help others at every stage or level of consciousness to learn of the wonders within.

She said of her husband: 'He was a practical mystic, possessed by the intellect of a scholar, the mind of a successful executive, the heart of the poet. His message summed up was: 'You are the king, the ruler of your world for you are one with God.'